"This is so relatable! It's speaking right into my life. I am in awe of Megan's honesty, transparency, and beautiful spirit."

— **Andrea Whitaker**, mother of two daughters

"La Follett engagingly shares Brother Lawrence's timeless truths with (sometimes) raw transparency - validating, guiding, and loving all who serve on the front lines of motherhood. If you believe in eating dessert first, begin with Megan's Letter #5."

— **Lynn Baber**, championship horse trainer and breeder, motivational speaker, and best-selling author of the Gospel Horse Series

The Practice of the Presence of God

for Modern-day Moms

by Megan La Follett

THUNDER & SILVER

All Scripture quotations taken from the New American Standard Bible® (NASB), Copyright © 1960, 1962, 1963, 1968, 1971, 1972, 1973, 1975, 1977, 1995 by The Lockman Foundation. Used by permission. www.Lockman.org

Paperback ISBN 978-0-9965106-4-6
eBook ISBN 978-0-9965106-5-3

Copyright © 2017 by Megan La Follett

Cover design by Ashlie Cook

All rights reserved. No part of this book may be reproduced or transmitted in any form or by any means, electronic or mechanical, including photocopying and recording, or by any information storage and retrieval system, without permission in writing from the publisher.

Published in the United States by Thunder & Silver, an imprint of Meraki Press, Houston.

Printed in the United States of America
2017 — First Edition

SPECIAL SALES
Quantity discounts are available for bulk purchases by churches or organizations. For information, please e-mail info@practicethepresence.com.

This book is dedicated to mothers
everywhere who need to know
that God is near,
right where they are,
as they are.

INTERVIEWS with and LETTERS from BROTHER LAWRENCE

on
the PRESENCE OF GOD*

The author of these Letters is Nicolas Hermann de Loraine, known as "Brother Lawrence" from the Order of the Discalced Carmelites in Paris.

This text which is reproduced here is a translation from a French version of the letters.

The Interviews seemed to have been preserved by Mr. Beaufort, vicar general of the Bishop of Chalons, under whose recommendation they were published. (He was the Cardinal of Noailles, who had become Archbishop of Paris in 1695). The Interviews are reprinted from a 1694 edition kept in the National Library in Paris.

(*) These texts are reproduced from a booklet (undated) published by "the Order of Watchers," a Protestant Order

First Interview
BROTHER LAWRENCE

The first time I saw Brother Lawrence, he told me that God had endowed him with a singular grace in his conversion when he was still out in the world at the age of eighteen. One day, as he was watching a leafless tree and thinking that it would soon grow leaves again, then blossom and bear fruit, he received a clear insight of the Providence and of God's Might, which had never left his soul since; and that insight lifted him completely from the world, and gave him such a love for God that he could not tell whether it has grown since then, more than forty years before.

He had been a footman for the treasurer of the Savings, a Mr. De Fieubert, and had been very clumsy and broke everything. He asked to enter religion and be admitted into a monastery, thinking he would be scathed for the blunders and mistakes he would make there, and that doing so, he would sacrifice his life and all its pleasures to God, but that God misled him, as he only found satisfaction there.

He told me that you have to surrender completely and purely to God, all that is temporal and spiritual, and delight in the fulfillment of His will, whether He lead us through pains or solace; everything has the same taste for a man who is really forsaken. You need faith in the arid and cold stretches of the soul, where God tries our love for Him.

It was then that you did the good deeds of resignation and abandonment, and you often had to go a long way for a single one of them.

In order to surrender to God as much as He expects us to, you have to watch carefully all moves from the soul in which spiritual matters and the crudest things mingle; God gives light accordingly to those who have the true desire to be His, and that if my wish was so, I could ask for Him whenever I wanted without fear of being a bother, but otherwise, I should let Him alone.

LETTERS from Megan La Follett

on
the PRESENCE OF GOD for MODERN-DAY MOMS

The author of these Letters is Megan Diane La Follett, from the Order of "Surviving is My Jam" in Houston, Texas.

First Letter
Megan La Follett

Dear Sister,

There's a small steepled church on top of the hill in my hometown, resting above the forested valleys. It wasn't my church, but I went to rummage sales there once or twice growing up, and marveled at the bare wood floors and hard pews. It wasn't until I was a mother visiting home that I attended a service on a whim with my father – and then only because he knew the service ended promptly at 11:00 and we had somewhere to be at 11:30.

    This time the sanctuary didn't feel outdated or stark. It radiated peace and community; a genuine striving toward…rest. No microphones or speakers or sound technicians. Simply the beauty of a cello played by an artist, lifting the sounds of praise with voices intermingled in familiar harmony.

    When I think about where I've felt the presence of God most clearly, this church comes to mind. An invitation to *be*, imperfect and broken and exhausted but it's okay because God can handle all of that.

Selah
(Pause & Reflect)

Second Interview
BROTHER LAWRENCE

Brother Lawrence told me he had always been governed by love, with no selfish concerns whatsoever. And since he had resolved that the love of God should be at the core of all his actions, he was satisfied with the outcome. He was happy to take a straw from the ground for the love of God, while genuinely looking for Him alone and not anything else, not even His gifts.

He had suffered greatly in his mind as he thought he was damned; no man in the world could have convinced him it was otherwise, but he had been able to reason about it as follows: I entered religion for the love of God alone, I strove to act for Him alone: whether I should be damned or saved, I want to keep on acting purely for the love of God. At least, I will have succeeded in doing all I could muster to love Him till I die.

This sorrow lasted four years, during which time he suffered much. But eventually, he realized this sorrow stemmed from a lack of faith, and since then, he had felt completely free and forever happy; he had put his sins between himself and God, as if to tell Him he did not deserve

His blessings, but it did not prevent God from granting them to him.

He learned that to begin with, you have to develop the habit of conversing continually with God, to tell Him all you did; but if you are diligent enough you will soon feel effortlessly awakened by His love.

He still expected to have his share of sorrow and suffering after all the good time God had granted him; but he did not worry about it, as he knew that since he could not do anything by himself, God would not fail to give him the strength to bear it.

When an opportunity to practice virtue arose, he would always address God saying: "Oh Lord, I cannot do this unless You make me do it, and He would grant him straight away the strength he needed, and even more."

When he failed, he but confessed his fault and told God: "I will never do anything else if you leave me; because I am absolutely determined to follow You, You have to prevent me from falling and to correct what is not right." Afterwards he would not worry about his fault, as he was sure God would forgive him.

You have to act very simply with God, and talk to Him honestly and ask His help with things as they come, and God will not fail to grant it; he had often experienced this himself.

He had been asked a few days back to go and stockpile Burgundy wine, which was very hard for him, because first he had no turn for business, but also because he was lame and the only way he could walk around the boat was by rolling over the casks. But he did not worry about that, nor about how he would buy the wine; he told God it was His business, after which he found everything was getting done and went on smoothly.

He had been sent to Auvergne the year before for the same business and he could not tell how the thing was done, and he was not the one who did it, but the thing was done and well done.

It was the same when it came to cooking, one of his greatest natural dislikes. He had grown used to doing his duty in the kitchen for the love of God, asking for His blessings on all occasions so as to get on with his task, and he had worked there with great ease for the fifteen years he had been employed there.

He was currently working at the second-hand shoe shop and he was very pleased with his position, but he was ready to leave it as he had left the other positions he occupied since he took pleasure everywhere he was by doing small things for the love of God.

For him the time allotted to prayers was in no way different from other times; he retired to pray when his superior asked him to, but he did not wish nor ask for it. His work, even the most demanding, could not divert him from God. As he knew he had to love God in all things and he endeavored to do so, he had no need for a supervisor, but rather a confessor to receive absolution for the sins he committed. He was very sensitive to his faults, but he did not let them discourage him. He would confess them to God and did not plead for Him to excuse them; but once this was done, he would peacefully resume his usual practice of love and adoration.

He had consulted no one in his sorrow; but with the light of faith, and the knowledge that God was present, he would simply act for Him, with the sole desire to please Him, and come what may.

Pointless thoughts can spoil everything—evil starts there; but we have to be careful and reject those thoughts as soon as we realize they are not relevant to our task at hand or our salvation, and resume our conversation with God which contents us.

At the beginning, all his time for prayers was spent rejecting pointless thoughts and relapsing into them again. Unlike the others, he had never been able to make it his duty to pray; all penance and such exercises were useful only in that they served to get united with God through love. After he had pondered over it, he realized that the shortest way to go straight to Him was through a continuous exercise of love, and to do everything for the love of God.

A great difference has to be made between the acts governed by *reason* and those governed by the *will*. The first are of little importance and the others are paramount. Unless you love God and rejoice in Him, you might well repent as much as you can; if it is not done with love, it will never wipe out a single sin.

We should, without anxiety, wait for the forgiveness of our sins by the blood of Jesus Christ, and strive to love Him with all our heart. Rather than choosing those who remained innocent, God seems to choose the greatest sinners to endow them with the greatest blessings, as thus His mercy is more poignant.

Second Letter
Megan La Follett

Dear Sister,

My husband's first post-grad-school job was in Florida. While there, I became a stay-at-home mom of two. It was a hard and a lonely time. But it gave me the chance to have daily tea with a friend and a neighbor who is one of the most deeply authentic and godly women I've met.

    A year later, we were living in Texas on a new leg of our adventure together. I was overwhelmed by three children under the age of four. But right across the street from our house was a church that offered childcare during Thursday morning studies. So I joined a Precepts study with a group of older women. I had never used inductive Bible study methods before—it shifted my practices and my perception of the Bible. I joined another, and another, hungry for meaty helpings of scripture. And these women were a safety blanket when I had my first battle with post-partum depression. They treated me with such grace and warmth, that I could feel God's presence through them.

I made some changes in my circumstances, self-care, getting "adult friend" time, better support, and I was doing better for a while. At least, I wasn't crying constantly.

But that was just a warning quake—the big earthquake was still coming.

A little less than a year after my third child was born, I entered into my "dark night of the soul." My spiritual habits were strong, my support system was in place, I was eating, exercising, sleeping well (for the first time since I became a mom). But I was shattered.

The depression twisted my thoughts into weapons that cut me into shreds. My vision was so "smudged" that everything looked like an enemy soldier. I wasn't sure what was real. I couldn't enjoy anything. I didn't want to be with my children. I couldn't *care* about anything.

When I met with a counselor for the first time, she asked me to rate my fear of being in her office on a scale of 1 to 10. I was more afraid to be there, where I would be forced to look at the depression straight on, than I was of death.

By June I was having panic attacks that landed me in the emergency room. My husband found me washing my hands over and over for minutes at the sink. Conflict would shut me down completely; I'd hug my knees, and my hands turned blue from rubbing my jeans.

On my 33rd birthday, I was admitted to a partial hospitalization program. I'd get up, have breakfast, then go to the center. At dinner time, I'd go home.

There was one thought, and one thought only, that carried me through. One wordless, primal prayer I held onto and cried continually to God. (This was when I really understood what continual prayer meant).

It was something like: "God, make something beautiful out of this. Make something that wouldn't be, if I didn't experience this."

And He has.

"Create in me a clean heart, O God,
and renew a right spirit within me.
Cast me not away from your presence,
and take not your Holy Spirit from me.
Restore to me the joy of your salvation,
and uphold me with a willing spirit."
Psalm 51:10-12

I came out the other side of the depression with a new spirit and a remade heart. I've found since then that I'm not satisfied by the same types of studies, the same activities. I feel a deeper, more direct call to work for His kingdom. I share my faith, my struggles, and my love for God more regularly and more intentionally with my children. I don't crumble under conflict.

Do I still have days where depression rears its ugly head? Yes. I think depression is like alcoholism in that way — I'm never going to be "recovered." It will always be a part of me. But so will Jesus, and together we can dance with it.

In your dark night of the soul, He is present.

For you shall go out in joy and be led forth in peace; the mountains and the hills before you shall break forth into singing, and all the trees of the field shall clap their hands.

Isaiah 55:12

Selah

Third Interview
BROTHER LAWRENCE

He told me that at the core of spiritual life in him had been the very high idea and esteem of God in itself, and once this idea was well conceived he had done nothing but reject dutifully all other thoughts at the beginning in order to act only for the love of God.

If a long time elapsed during which he did not think of Him, it would not trouble him. But after he had confessed his misery to God, he returned to Him with so much confidence in Him that he felt wretched for having forsaken Him.

The trust we have in God honors Him greatly, and attracts great blessings on us.

It is impossible for God to make a mistake, even when He lets a soul completely devoted to Him and resolved to endure anything for His sake, suffer a great deal.

He had managed to have no other thoughts except the thoughts of God. So often he had experienced the prompt assistance of God in every occasion that when he had to do business outside, he did not ponder over it in advance, but when it was time to act, he saw in God as in a clear mirror what he had to do for the occasion; he had acted thus with no anticipation whatsoever for some time now.

Before experiencing the prompt assistance of God in his business, he had resorted to his foresight; now he was much more united to God in his everyday activities than when he left them aside to retreat and pray God.

He expected to suffer greatly in his body or his mind and that his worst fear was to lose that sense of God which had been in him for so long, but that God's Mercy would comfort him. He would never abandon him completely and He would give him the strength to endure the pain. He would allow this to happen to him; thus he feared nothing and had no need to talk about his soul to anyone. When he had attempted to do so, he had always felt more uneasy afterwards.

Knowing he was ready to sacrifice his life for the love of God, he did not fear danger, and the safest way, with always enough light to know our whereabout, was to surrender completely to God.

You have to be faithful to your wish to act and surrender yourself in the beginning, but afterwards, it is only unutterable joy. In the throe of difficulties, you must resort to Jesus Christ and beg for his blessing, with which everything became easy.

He said that we stuck to penance and specific exercises, while leaving aside Love which is the goal; this was clearly visible in the works, and was the reason why so little solid virtue could be seen.

Neither delicacy nor science are necessary to go to God, only a heart determined to beat and care for Him and Him alone, and to love Him alone.

Third Letter
Megan La Follett

Dear sister,

If you look at my husband's computer and my computer at any given time, you'll notice one big difference. He will have one, *maybe* up to three, browser tabs open… and I'll have three different browsers with twenty tabs open. Each.

That's about how my brain looks most of the time too.

And I have a confession. My calendars (yes, plural) are the same.

My "mom" calendar is supposed to have everything, but sometimes I miss information from one of my many sources:

- My husband's calendar
- The preschool calendar
- The elementary school calendar
- Church calendar
- My work calendar
- Meal planning calendar
- Marital "staff" calendar

- Childcare schedule for my youngest
- Homeschool calendar for my eldest
- And, of course, the calendar of movies playing at the Alamo Drafthouse Cinema.

Ever week, I spend Sunday evening trying to make all of these fit.

That's enough "tabs" to crash a top-of-the-line computer. Black screen of death, with one blinking word: OVERWHELM.

How to make sure everything gets done that must be done, without "overwhelm" ruling my life?

Vacations offer a respite—sometimes. Definitely not during that two-year period where every vacation in my family involved someone vomiting (or "yodeling in technicolor, as my childhood bosom friend used to call it). Enjoy a day trip to the beach…two boys taking turns throwing up all the way home. Family vacation in the mountains, one constantly vomiting daughter. A ten-year anniversary cruise while five months pregnant, a never-to-be-forgotten bout of norovirus. No respite in those years.

Retreats are better. Every year, I head out to Texas hill country with my community from church. Next to the river, following a blessed night of uninterrupted sleep, it is easy to draw deeply from the well and be, for a time, free of the hold of a calendar.

After such a time, the danger is that I'll return home convinced I can take control of my calendar. I can apply more productivity tactics or find another app that will finally do the trick. I can plan *better*.

But what about when I'm in the middle of the mess, When the very thought of retreat seems a cruel joke?

When planning fails. When a cold, a flu, and a stomach bug rotate through all six members of my family in three weeks?

Efficiency, productivity, and planning are all good. But they can't connect me to God. Better planning, a perfected mom calendar, may reduce the distractions of messy life.

They turn down the noise, clear the land.

Surrender in the middle of the mess strengthens the signal.

Instead of: PLAN BETTER.

God wants me to: REST IN THE MESS.

Keep turning my mind and my heart to the source of rest. Tune into the signal of God's presence. See my world through a #GodFilter.

The calendars aren't going away. The presence of God defeats their power to overwhelm.

In the mob of thoughts and the "mom calendar" **He is present.**

May the God of hope fill you with all peace and joy as you trust in him so that you overflow with hope by the power of the Holy Spirit.

Romans 15:13

Selah

Fourth Letter
BROTHER LAWRENCE

Today, I received two books and a letter from Sister***, who is getting ready for her profession. For the occasion, she wishes to have the prayers from your Orders and particularly yours. I reckon she relies heavily on those prayers; pray let us not disappoint her.

Ask God to make her capable of doing this sacrifice so as to get His love alone and be strongly determined to be fully devoted to Him. I will send you one of these books about the presence of God, a topic which, in my opinion, deals with spiritual life as a whole, and it seems to me that whoever diligently practices this presence of God will soon become highly spiritual.

I know that in order to practice it well, the heart has to be empty of all other things, because God wants to possess our heart alone. Just as He can possess it alone only if we empty it of all that is not His, He can act and do what He would like to only if the place is left vacant for Him.

There is no life sweeter and more delightful than a life of continuous conversation with God; only those who practice and experience it can understand it. However, I do not advise you to choose this life on that account.

It is not pleasure that we ought to seek in this exercise; we must do it on a principle of love and because God wishes to have us.

If I were a preacher, I would preach for the practice of the presence of God above all things; and if I were a father confessor, I would advise it to everyone because I think it is both necessary and easy.

If only we knew how much we need God's blessing and support, we would never lose sight of Him, not even for a second. Believe me and make immediately the holy and strong resolution to never forget God willingly, and to spend the rest of your life in His holy presence, deprived, for the love of Him if He deems it fit, of all solace.

Get about this work with all your heart, and if you do it as you ought to, be assured that you will soon feel the effects. I will assist you with my prayers, insignificant as they are. I recommend myself to yours and those of your Order, being theirs and more particularly

Yours, etc.

Fourth Letter
Megan La Follett

Dear sister,

As I encourage you to practice the presence of God, I fear I may focus too much on the *present*. The fullness of His presence, eternal and unbound, cannot be experienced in the present alone.

The most we can hope for or endure is a glimpse of His fullness while we live in time—but there is more to that glimpse if we are present with Him in the past and in the future as well as in this one moment, this one finite breath of *now*.

Our hearts, minds, and even bodies exist in more than one state. The past is written in all of them.

The future—how we see it, fear it, hope for it—determines what we do with them.

If I am persuaded that running two miles a day will mean the difference between meeting my grandchildren or not, that will change my present choices.

If I broke an ankle last month, that will change my options for exercising today.

Just so, I *am* persuaded by the power of the Holy Spirit that God is a God of hope. That means He *has* me. Nothing, and no amount of time or state of existence, can separate me from His love.

As I look for His presence in the present, I must also seek Him in the past and in the future.

We're called to 3-D living.

Seeing God's presence in the past, trusting His presence in my future, changes *everything* in my present.

I have an app on my phone that pulls pictures and status updates from my social media accounts, showing me moments from one year ago, two years ago, and so on. After the GPS map directions (and the Starbucks mobile order app), this is my favorite feature on my phone. Oh—and the whole "calling people" function…

Seeing my nine-year-old daughter back when she had tiny, tight golden curls and played golf in our backyard while wearing a Cinderella dress…it catches my breath and stills my heart.

Then I glance around to see what she's doing right now. I notice her more. I am more present with her.

And I think, seven years from now, what a picture of *this* moment will do to me.

Nothing in the present could distract me from my daughter. Not in that moment. She has all of me.

I urge you to find a way to record the times you see the hand of God at work. Record it in a way that you can easily come back to it. If you are musical, write or find a song to hold that moment still in time. If you are an artist, keep a portfolio of #GodScapes. If you love numbers, keep a spreadsheet with details and dates.

Knit it, write it, dance it, carve it into wood.

So that it will be there to enrich your experience of God's presence in your future presents.

Each January, I sit down at a coffee shop and rebel against resolutions. I write out five things—just things, big or small, important or not—that I want to do in the coming year. Then five things I want to do within five years.

Before I start, though, I write out how old each of my children will be at the end of five years, how many years of marriage we'll be celebrating, where I think I might be living.

Five years...

> Aurelia – 14 years old – 9th grade
> Blaise – 11 years old – 6th grade
> Maxwell – 9 years old – 4th grade
> Philip – 6 years old – 1st grade
> 20 years of marriage
> I'll be 40 years old

I have to breathe that in. Let the picture of that future settle in my soul before I can continue.

None of that reality is guaranteed, of course. But intentionally and actively putting myself in that place changes my perspective. I choose different "five things" than I would have five minutes earlier.

Again, I am more aware of and connected to my 9-year old daughter today after I've spent time visiting my 14-year old daughter in the future.

This is what I mean by "3-D Living."

The Holy Spirit and the promises in scripture point us towards our future with God. He has laid eternity in the heart of man and woman.

When my time on earth ends, He will take the past, present, and future of my life and wrap them around me and make me whole.

Only then can I be fully present with Him. In the meantime, I encourage you, along with me, to reach for that vision of eternity by practicing in the past, in the present, and in the future.

In the past, the present, and the future –
In every moment
and state of your heart
He is present

He has made everything beautiful in its time. He has also set eternity in the human heart.

Ecclesiastes 3:11

 # Selah

Fifth Letter
Brother Lawrence

I received from Mrs. *** the objects you gave her for me. I am surprised you do not share your thoughts on the little book I sent you which you should have received. Be diligent, I pray you. in practicing it with all your heart in your old age, as it is better late than never.

I cannot fathom how religious people can be satisfied in life without the practice of the presence of God. For my part, I live secluded with Him in the depths and the heart of my soul as much as I can; and while I am thus with Him, I fear nothing; but the slightest move away from Him is unbearable to me.

This exercise does not exhaust the body. However it is good to deprive the body sometimes, often even, of so many innocent little pleasures legitimate in themselves, because God would not tolerate that a soul who wants to be utterly devoted to Him could find pleasures elsewhere but in Him; this is more than reasonable.

I don't mean here that we should impose a severe constraint on ourselves. No, we should serve God in a holy freedom, we should do our duty faithfully, without anxiety nor worry, and bring our mind back to God quietly and calmly whenever we catch it wandering far from Him.

However, we must put all our trust in God and get rid of all worries, and even of many specific kinds of devotion which are good in themselves but which weigh on us uselessly because eventually these devotions are but a means to get to the end. And so, if by this exercise of the presence of God we are with Him who is our end, it is useless to get back to the means; but we can continue to trade love with Him, and stay in His Holy presence sometimes by an act of submission, and in all the ways our minds can think of.

Don't be discouraged by the reluctance you can feel in the flesh; you have to do yourself violence. At first, we often think it is a waste of time; but you must persevere and be determined to persevere in these things till death, in spite of all the difficulties that may arise.

I recommend myself to the prayers of your Order and yours in particular. I am, in our Lord

Yours, etc.

Fifth Letter
Megan La Follett

Dear Sister,

As a grad-student mom, as a stay-at-home mom, as a work-from-home mom, and as a part-time office mom…I speak from experience that the idea of regular spiritual practices seems at best a fairytale and at worst a source of guilt and failure.

Prayer, silence, solitude, fasting…

I can't even use the bathroom unattended by need and noise.

This is where the monks have got a *distinct* advantage!

Praise God that He seeks us in the noise, because I can't find the volume button.

Jesus showed us how to live—but he did not, *does* not, expect the ministry of a mother to look like the ministry of a first-century single, childless rabbi.

Hear this.

God gives us *rest*. He commands us to love Him and love one another, and to make disciples as we go. He came to set you FREE from sin—and free, oh-so free, from condemnation.

The classic spiritual practices can help us see, touch, hear, and understand God more.

When they are done in the power of the Holy Spirit, out of a heart of obedience and a desire to seek God's face.

They are meant as a gift, a set of tools.

If a tool isn't doing the work it is intended for, if it is rubbing your hands raw, you should *put it down.*

Tools — spiritual habits — are meant to aid you, not harm you.

[SIDEBAR: Yes, it takes discipline to establish a spiritual habit, and you may need to use a tool for a period of time to learn to use it well and build callouses. Pushing hard into it can lead to transformational practices. To learn more about spiritual disciplines, visit www.practicethepresence/habits.]

Nothing — not noise, chaos, sibling arguments over imaginary worlds, or sleep deprivation — can separate you from the love of God.

Check your heart. Ask the Holy Spirit to reveal to you if trying to fit a particular spiritual habit into your current stage of life and ministry is actually keeping you from experiencing the presence of God. Fight for it. Don't let the practice get in the way of the *point* of that practice.

I can't close this letter without making a clear statement about the ministry of motherhood.

The most important disciples in your life are your children. Period. But in my experience of American Christian culture, there are two widespread lies about parenting that you need to guard against.

Lie #1: You are responsible for raising little kingdom-builders.

Thank God, the salvation of my children does not fall to me. Never does Jesus say, MAKE the little children look like me. He says to bring the little children to him. *Let* them come to him.

Just like you, your amazing, incredible, and beloved child will make choices dishonoring to God (and to you). You cannot bear their guilt. Jesus does that. Don't dishonor *him* by trying to take his place on the cross.

Lie #2: No one will argue that a 21st century mom can live a life similar to the daily reality of a 17th century monk in Paris, much less a carpenter's son in first century Israel. But you will hear the claim that there is *one* way to live your life as a mother raising children in a godly manner.

The exact details will differ depending on your community, but I dare you to write out what the "ideal" mother looks like in your church.

It is probably quite lovely.

It is definitely crushing the spirit of at least a portion of the women trying to fit that ideal. If not *all* of them.

You have a unique set of natural strengths, spiritual gifts, and personality traits. Only because God is so astoundingly vast can each of us be a completely one-of-a-kind reflection of His image. Every individual who has ever been born, if you add us all together, even that many reflections of God can't come close to His full image!

God wants you to be fully alive.

You can minister to your family and never bake a cupcake.

You can raise your children and show them Jesus without ever doing the laundry!

Heresy, you say?

Sure, you may have to do the laundry and clean the toilets because of your circumstances in life. And the good and excellent news I have for you (and me) is that God is there in the laundry room and when you're wearing the yellow rubber gloves and whenever you change the baby's diaper. Oh, He is THERE.

My dear sister, what I'm saying is if you are exercising your strengths in a calling that happens to create the circumstance that you pay someone else to be there, you can still be ministering to your "first" disciples. God is there too.

Where the noise overwhelms,
and practice seems impossible,
He is present.

The thief comes only to steal and kill and destroy; I come that they may have life, and have it abundantly.

John 10:10

Selah

Sixth Letter
Brother Lawrence

I pity you much. It is highly important that you leave your business to the care of *** and spend the rest of your life worshiping God. He does not require great things from us, simply that you remember Him, worship Him, and address Him a prayer to get His blessing; that you sometimes offer your sufferings to Him or that you thank Him for the favors he has done and keeps on doing you in the midst of your turmoil, and that you manage to find solace by His side as often as you can.

Raise your heart to him, even during your meals and when you are surrounded with people. You do not need to cry out loud. He is closer to us than what we think; there is no need to be always at church to be with God. We can turn our heart into an oratory where we retreat to converse with Him meekly, humbly and with love. All of us can have these intimate conversations with God, some more, some less; He knows what we are capable of. Let us begin then.

Maybe He is just expecting from us a good resolution. Let us gather our courage. We have but little time left to live, you are nearly sixty-four and I am almost eighty. Let us live and die with God. Our sufferings will be sweet and pleasant if we are with Him; while the greatest pleasures would be a cruel punishment without Him. May he be blessed for all that is! Amen.

Get used to worshiping Him, to asking for his blessing, and to offering Him your heart from time to time while going about your business, and any time if you can.

Do not always stick strictly to rules or some specific forms of devotion; but live with trust in God and act with love and humility. You can count on my meager prayers, and be assured that I am your servant in our Lord.

Sixth Letter

Megan La Follett

Dear Sister,

When I was in high school, I finally had to admit that I needed glasses. I'll never forget the first time I put those glasses on and looked at the trees behind my house. Startled, I turned and asked my mother if there had always been birds in the trees. I could actually *see* the leaves, and how the wind moved them individually and all together at the same time.

That's what worship does. It clarifies our vision so we can see Him. It's like scales dropping from your eyes. But you have to be the one to put on the lenses. He will not force Himself on you.

One of the best spiritual teachers I've ever had, Dr. Steve Jones, asked once why Jesus spoke in parables. The usual answers came up in the group; story is powerful, parables make high concepts accessible, illustrations make spiritual truth easier to understand. That's not the answer Jesus gave when the disciples asked him (see Matthew 13:10-17).

This is what Jesus said:

"Otherwise they would see with their eyes, hear with their ears, and understand with their heart and return, and I would heal them."

Isn't that contrary to everything we know about Jesus? Does he *not* desire for each of us to return and be healed? At first glance, this passage of scripture seems to indicate that he spoke in parables to obscure the truth and prevent people from understanding with their hearts!

Let us look deeper, for we can be assured that this is not the case.

If Jesus revealed the truth clearly to people who were not seeking him, he would be forcing himself on them. The truth would be so blindingly brilliant that, even with their eyes closed, they would see it clearly. And then they would have no choice. Their free will would be shattered. Instead of a marriage, it would be unwilling intimacy.

Even before we know of our sin, God seeks us. But before He can heal us and restore our hearts to worship Him, we must seek Him in return.

Retreat into the oratory of your heart and receive willingly the truth the Holy Spirit imparts to you there. Recall the joy you feel when your difficult child hugs you or leaves you a love note. Just so, offer God your heart from time to time while going about your business.

If you build a worship center in your heart, **you will see Him.**

He has told you, O man, what is good; And what does the Lord require of you But to do justice, to love kindness, And to walk humbly with your God?

Micah 6:8

 Selah

Seventh Letter
Brother Lawrence

About wandering thoughts in prayers.

You are not telling me anything new; you are not the only one to be distracted by your thoughts in your prayers. Our mind is a great wanderer; but since the most important of our faculties is our will, it has to call it back and bring it back to God.

When our mind, for want of being sufficiently disciplined by contemplation in the first days of our devotion, has entered into some bad habits of distraction and dissipation, it is very difficult to overcome them, and they usually draw us towards earthly matters, even against our will.

I believe that a remedy for this is to confess our faults and to humble ourselves before God. I do not advise you to use a great many words in your prayers, as many words and long speeches are often what triggers distraction.

Stand praying before God like a lame and dumb beggar at the gate of a wealthy man. Make it your first concern to keep your mind in the presence of God. If it sometimes wanders and errs far from Him, do not worry too much about that; worries and anxiety are but a way to distract the mind rather than collect it. The will must simply bring it back to God, and if you so persevere, God will have mercy on you.

A sure way to have a quiet and collected mind when the time for prayer comes is not to let it wander anytime; you should always keep it strictly in the presence of God. Then, when you are used to thinking about Him often, you will find it easy to keep a peaceful mind at the time of prayer, or at least, to call it back if it is distracted.

I have already told you in my previous letters about the benefits that we can draw from this practice of the presence of God; let us get on with it seriously and pray for one another.

Yours, etc.

Seventh Letter
Megan La Follett

Dear Sister,

As much as I wish it wasn't so, I am sure I'm not alone in having a strong streak of perfectionism. If I can't do something well, my first instinct is to hit "restart."

Just so, in my attempts at prayer, if my mind wanders, I feel like a failure. Slowly, at a speed that makes a glacier seem like a victorious Formula 1 race car, I am learning that #FailureIsFeedback.

The feedback I've received from my prayer fails, and that I encourage you to apply to your own life, is that simple prayer is made possible by doing some work ahead of time. Set up a system to trigger your mind to return to prayerfulness.

Set markers in your life to signal your will to gather up your wandering mind and return it to prayer. Allow yourself to be humbled, by accepting the need for these "markers."

They do not need to be complicated things. You can use the natural rhythm of your day, simply by choosing to be more intentional and present.

I've failed miserably at instituting scheduled times to pray with my children. But on the way to school every day, we sit at a red light. I use that traffic signal as a marker. When we pull up at the end of the line, we start our "Stop Light Prayer." It has become such an integral part of morning that if it takes me more than a moment to begin praying, my children remind me.

My body's signals can serve as a marker. When I can't breathe because of anxiety or the sheer noise and chaos of many children in a home, I find a space to sit and do breathing exercises. Five seconds breathing in. Five seconds hold. Five seconds breathing out. And while I breathe, I pray.

The central ingredients of gratitude are humility (knowing your mind will wander), devotion (desiring to connect with God), and joy (rejoicing in the goodness of God who delivers us). The actions required are to stop (be present), feel (His nearness), and know (His goodness).

If your will brings your wandering mind back to God in simple prayer, you will see Him.

Therefore repent and return, so that your sins may be wiped away, in order that times of refreshing may come from the presence of the Lord.

Acts 3:19

Selah

Eighth Letter
BROTHER LAWRENCE

Here enclosed is the answer to the letter I received from ***; be so kind as to hand it to her. She seems full of good will, but she would like to go faster than Grace itself. You cannot become a saint overnight. I recommend her to you. We need to help one another through our mutual advice and by setting a good example. I would be grateful if you could let me know about her from time to time, and tell me if she is really devout and obedient.

Let us not forget by this that our sole duty in this life is to please God, and apart from that, everything is but madness and vanity. You and I have lived for about forty years in a monastic life.

Have we used these years to love and serve God who asked us to live this life and for this end? I feel ashamed and confused when I reflect on the great favors God granted me and keeps on granting me on the one hand, and on the ill use I make of them and the little progress I make towards perfection on the other hand.

Since He grants us some more time in His mercy, let us set to work sincerely, make up for the time we lost and return with self-confidence to our Father of full of mercy who is always willing to receive us with kindness. Let us relinquish liberally all that is not His for His sake; He deserves so much more. Let us think of Him consistently. Let us trust Him with all our heart. I have no doubt we will soon see the effects and receive the blessing He dispenses lavishly, with which we can do anything, and without which we can do nothing but sin.

We cannot escape the dangers that are legion in Life without God's active and steady help; let us ask for it at all times. How can we pray to Him if we are not with Him? And how can we be with Him if we don't think of Him often? And how can we think of Him often unless we pick up this holy habit?

You will say I keep saying the same thing over and over again. It is true, because it is the best and the easiest method I know; and since I do not use any other, this is the method I recommend to everyone. It is necessary to know before being able to love. In order to know God, we must think of Him often, and when we love Him, we will also think of Him often, because our heart will be where our wealth is. This argument is well worth our consideration.

I am yours, etc.

Eighth Letter
Megan La Follett

Dear Sister,

For four years, I devoted myself to scientific research in graduate school. During that time, I had my first two children. I did not complete my degree. It was left, unfinished, as we moved across the country and started a life in a different state.

You can imagine the problem this was for a recovering perfectionist. The years surrounding that unfinished ending were infused with madness and vanity. Madness: motherhood defining me. Vanity: a degree defining me.

In the end, I believe that it was my faults that revealed the world's madness and cleared the way to knowing God more deeply. Perhaps that is part of the meaning of the mystery of Paul's statement that "when I am weak, then I am strong." (2 Corinthians 12:10)

If I had completed my degree as planned, if I had been a perfect stay-at-home mother, I would not have seen the madness and vanity and thus be able to dismiss it as such. Instead, to find my purpose in pleasing God. To know Him, to think of Him, to love Him; regardless of whether I was an acclaimed scientist or an unseen mother.

I actually had multiple people scoff at my choice to stay at home after working so long on a doctorate. It was a waste, they said, as they shook their heads in grave disappointment. Madness.

Years later, I experienced the opposite when I chose to work outside the home. How could I leave my children in the care of another? It was a shame, they said, for me to make such a selfish choice. Vanity, if I had allowed these words to decide my path.

God has a plan for this world, and it does not matter to this plan if I am a scientist or a mother or I stay at home or I go to work. That is the height of hubris. It matters only that I know Him, think of Him, and love Him.

This will not happen overnight. One doesn't become a mother in an instant – not at the moment of conceiving a baby, not at the moment of birth. You become a mother continually, understanding more each day about what that means. So it is with becoming a saint.

When you see everything else as madness and vanity,
you will see Him.

Therefore let us draw near with confidence to the throne of grace, so that we may receive mercy and find grace to help in time of need.

Hebrews 4:16

 # Selah

Ninth Letter
BROTHER LAWRENCE

I had a hard time to bring myself to write, and I am doing it now only because you and Mrs.*** wish me to. Please write the address on the letter and send it to her. I am delighted in the trust you have in God; I wish He would make this trust grow in you even more. We cannot have too much trust in such a good and faithful friend that will never give up on us, neither in this world nor in the next.

If Mr. *** makes up for the loss he experienced and places all his trust in God, God will soon give him another friend even better. He deals with the hearts as he likes.

Maybe Mr.*** was too much attached to the one he lost. We must love our friends, but this love should not encroach on the love for God, which should be our first priority.

Pray, remember what I recommended to you; that is, to think of God often, by day and by night, while you go about your business, and even when you relax. He is always near you and with you. Do not leave Him alone.

You would not dare leave a friend visiting you alone; so why should God be thus neglected? And so do not forget Him, but think of Him often, worship Him constantly, live and die for Him; such is the glorious business of a Christian.

Besides, this is our purpose; if we don't know it, we have to learn it. I will strive to help you with my prayers. I am in our Lord, yours, etc.

Ninth Letter
Megan La Follett

Dear Sister,

How do you know when someone has become a spiritual friend? When you care for the connection more than you fear judgement? When you can share a burden with her as easily as shoulder a burden from her?

When midnight comes, and you're nursing alone with a baby who requires life from you, and you think of Jesus in the garden at Gethsemane and the sleeping disciples who left him alone in his agony — when a name comes to mind and you send out a text, that is the intimacy of true friendship. A relief and a joy to have a "3 AM friend."

I entreat you to pursue a friend like this. One who, unlike Jesus, will fail you, but will go to the garden at midnight with you. A kindred spirit who falls and bears scrapes and scars, but will be there to offer a hand when you do the same. Who sings with you praises for today and prayers for tomorrow.

There is no greater power on earth than a spiritual friend to aid you in turning your mind back to God. The Holy Spirit is the first and foremost of these friends, but you are meant to grow with other spirits who were created in God's image.

There are no ordinary people. Find the image of God in each person you meet, and when you find a reflection that resonates with yours, then live out His image together as you grow to be more than a marred mirror but rather a restored, living image of Christ.

> *"You have never talked to a mere mortal. Nations, cultures, arts, civilizations – these are mortal, and their life is to ours as the life of a gnat. But it is immortals whom we joke with, work with, marry, snub, and exploit – immortal horrors or everlasting splendors."* C.S. Lewis, The Weight of Glory

Pursue the extraordinary in the people you meet, and you will see Him.

And those who know Your name will put their trust in You, For You, O Lord, have not forsaken those who seek You.

Psalm 9:10

Selah

Tenth Letter
Brother Lawrence

About poor health.

I do not pray so that you be delivered from your pains; but I pray God sincerely so that He gives you the strength and patience to endure them as long as He wishes. Strengthen yourself in Him who holds you bound to the Cross. He will untie you when He seems fit. Blessed are those who suffer with Him! Get accustomed to suffer in such manner, and seek in Him the strength to endure it as much and as long as He deems it necessary for you to.

The great people in the world do not understand these truths, and it is no wonder because they suffer like socialites and not like Christians. They view illness as a suffering for the flesh and not as a favor from God; and since they see it only in that light, they find nothing in it but sorrow and despair. But those who receive the illness from the hand of God, and perceive it as the effect of His mercy and the means He uses for their salvation, usually find a great sweetness and a real solace in it.

I wish you would be able to convince yourself that God is often (in a way) closer to us, and more really present with us when we are sick than when we are in health. Whatever the remedies you take, they will succeed only to the extent He allows them to. When the pains come from God, He is the only one who can cure them. He often sends diseases to the body so as to save us from the diseases of the soul. Take solace in the Supreme physician of the soul and the body. Be satisfied with the condition God grants you.

Even though you may think I am happy, I envy you in fact. Pains and sufferings would be heaven to me if I suffered with my God; and the greatest pleasures would be hell, if I was to enjoy them without Him. My only solace would be to suffer from something in His name.

I am bound to go to God shortly. The delight I get in this life is that I see Him through faith; and I see Him in such a way that I could sometimes say: "I no longer believe, but I do see." I have the feeling that faith is what teaches us and, with this absolute certainty and this practice of faith, I want to live and die with Him.

And thus persevere with God always: He is the only comfort, the only solace for your affliction. I will beseech Him to be with you. Please accept my warmest greetings.

Yours, etc.

Tenth Letter
Megan La Follett

Dear Sister,

I shared with you in an earlier letter my battle with depression. This is the deepest suffering I have endured, and it was only after I accepted the suffering and worshipped God in it that my doctor found a treatment that freed me from it. For that, I am grateful. For in that pain, I was able to find solace in the knowledge that God would (and did) make something beautiful come out of it. I hope, and pray, that I will not soon forget this lesson.

And yet, this is a topic I continue to struggle with. Human suffering and God's compassion seem wholly incompatible, even though I've seen His compassion in the middle of the suffering. It only makes any sense if we know that God suffers with us. Jesus wept—sad and angry weeping. He was identifying with his friends. His lamentation was an act of worship.

It only makes sense if the suffering isn't the end of the story. We have hope that we will be free of it someday, and that in the meantime we can continue to trust in God's goodness. We can allow the pain to help us understand, down deep in our bones, the incredible sacrifice Jesus made on the cross to take on our suffering. Perhaps that hope will be fulfilled by a new medication, or a surgery, or treatment, or a miracle. Perhaps the suffering will remain until we are given a new body in heaven, and our minds and souls are restored through completed fulfillment in Christ.

Have the courage to lament and cry out for solace. Invite someone into your lamentation.

In the solace in the suffering,
you will see Him.

For just as the sufferings of Christ are ours in abundance, so also our comfort is abundant through Christ.

2 Corinthians 1:5

Selah

Eleventh letter
Brother Lawrence

To a sick man.

If we were better accustomed to practice the presence of God, all physical diseases would thus be much alleviated as God often allows us to suffer a little to purify our souls and to compel us to persevere with him.

Be courageous and offer Him your sufferings constantly, ask Him for the strength to endure them. Above all, get into the habit of conversing often with God, and try to forget Him as little as possible. Worship Him in all your infirmities, give yourself to Him every now and then; and at the height of your sufferings, beseech Him humbly and lovingly (as a child to his father) to make you comply with His holy will. I will try to help you with my meager prayers.

God has many ways to draw us to Him. Sometimes He hides from us; but faith alone, which will never fail us when we need it, must be our support and the founding principle of our trust, which must be all in God. I do not know how God shall deal with me; but I am always happy. The whole world is suffering; and I, who deserves the most severe discipline, feel a joy so constant and so great that I can hardly contain it.

I would willingly ask God for a share of your sufferings but I know that my weakness is so great that, should He leave me a single moment by myself, I would be the most wretched man. And yet I cannot fathom how God could leave me, because faith convinces me that He will never forsake us as long as we don't forsake Him in the first place. Let us fear to leave Him. Let us be always with Him. Let us live and die in His presence. Do you pray for me as I pray for you?

I am yours, etc.

Eleventh Letter
Megan La Follett

Dear Sister,

I am convinced that God sometimes seems distant because He wishes to reveal what else we have faith in, and we suffer until our faith is driven to Him. I would go so far as to say that part of the grace in this broken world is that the natural consequences of our sins point us to Him.

As a young girl, I read *The Chronicles of Narnia* at least once a year for many years. There are many gems of truth to be mined from these stories, but the most enduring story for me is the restoration of Eustace in *The Voyage of the Dawn Treader*.

If you recall (or if not, you must go find a copy and read it today), Eustace Scrubb was quite a horrible person when he was pulled into his first adventure in Narnia. His selfishness and contempt for others literally led him astray, until he was lost in a valley inhabited by a dragon. To his great fortune, the dragon died as he arrived. A driving rainstorm made him seek shelter in the dragon's den, where with a heart full of greed and selfish thoughts, he put on a golden armband from the treasure hoard. When he awoke, the magic of Narnia had transformed him into a dragon.

While my seven-year-old son is quite sure this would be a wonderful thing, it was terrible for Eustace. It changed him into a better person, but it seemed as if he had no hope. Does this not sound familiar?

His rescue came in an encounter with Aslan, who symbolizes Jesus. Had he not endured the suffering of being changed into a dragon, he would not have been ready or able to see Aslan. In this encounter, Eustace was told to remove his skin and step into a well. Three times he did this, but each time he went down to the well he saw in his reflection that he was still a rough, wrinkled, scaly dragon.

How often do we try, and try, and try again to rid ourselves of our sinful nature? But we cannot reach nearly deep enough.

Eustace was so desperate to be free of his dragon skin, that he overcame his fear of the lion's claws and allowed Aslan to undress him. Then Aslan threw him into the well water, and Eustace was restored.

Only Christ Jesus can change our very nature. Do not seek suffering, but when it comes, look for what is keeping you from Him.

When you have no hope but Jesus,
You will see Him.

These things I have spoken to you so that My joy may be in you, and that your joy may be made full.

John 15:11

Selah

Twelfth Letter
Brother Lawrence

To the same,

I am sorry to hear you've been suffering for so long; what comforts me and softens the feelings I entertain as regards your pains is that they demonstrate how much love God has for you. Look upon them from this perspective, and you will bear them more easily. My opinion is that, in your case, you should put aside human remedies and resort entirely to Divine Providence. Maybe He is only expecting from you this resignation and a perfect trust in Him to cure you. Since, in spite of all your treatments, medicine has proved powerless and your disease is getting worse, it wouldn't be tempting God to surrender yourself into His hands and to expect everything from Him.

I told you in my last letter that He sometimes resorts to physical diseases in order to cure spiritual ailments. And so be brave. Make a virtue of necessity. Require from God, not to be relieved from your pains, but strength to bear resolutely all He would burden you with for the love of Him.

Such prayers are indeed hard for the flesh, but all the more pleasant to God and sweet for those who love Him. Love softens the pain; and when we love God, we suffer for the sake of God with joy and courage. Let it be so for you I implore you. Find solace by His side; as He is the physician of all our diseases. He is the Father of the afflicted and is always ready to assist. He loves us so much more than what we think; let us love Him then, and do not seek solace elsewhere. I hope you will receive it soon.

Farewell. I will help you with my prayers, insignificant as they may be, and will always be in our Lord.

Yours, etc.

Twelfth Letter
Megan La Follett

Dear Sister,

Maybe you shouldn't be a mommy. Those words, from my daughter, cut straight to my heart. She'd just spoken my deepest fear.

She was right—I was a wretched mother. But the definition of "wretched" isn't "bad." It means exhausted, spent, someone who has been on the battlefield and has nothing left. I could not enjoy being with my children. There's a difference between the "survival is my jam" phase of motherhood (it genuinely does get easier, moms of littles!), and living in near-constant fear of the next thing your children need from you because there is no "you" left.

But if I didn't do it, who would? I lived by the philosophy that if it has to be done, do it. Whatever the cost to yourself.

If you are at the end of yourself, speak it. Face it. Let the Holy Spirit pray for you when you have no words. Hold onto one prayer, the prayer that never fails – He will transform you.

Experiencing, *enjoying*, God isn't dependent on serotonin levels or a good night's sleep. He is THERE.

That doesn't, however, mean that He wants me to STAY there. He offers rest to the weary, hope to the broken-hearted. His yoke is easy and His burden is light.

He made beautiful things out of my darkness (sound familiar? Genesis 1?), and continues to do that when the heavy clouds gather. But I also learned, through my pastor's teachings, from my counselor, with the support of my church community, how to care for myself better so He could flow through me, and not just to me.

It takes immense courage, dear sister, to trust the relief of your burden to another—even to God. You don't have to do everything. He will give you strength to do what He requires of you. If your strength is spent, and there is more to do, it is not meant for you to do it; or you are doing what is meant for another.

Where He is, there is resolute strength.

Trust in the Lord forever,
For in God the Lord, we have an everlasting Rock.

Isaiah 26:4

 # Selah

Thirteenth Letter
BROTHER LAWRENCE

To the same.

I praise God for the relief he has granted you according to your wish. I have often been close to death, but I have never been as happy as I was then. That is why I didn't pray to get relief, but in order to be strong enough to suffer with courage, humility and love. Ah! How sweet it is to suffer with God! No matter how great your sufferings are, accept them with love.

It is heaven to suffer with Him; that is why we must get used to an intimate, humble and loving conversation with Him in this life if we want to enjoy peace in Heaven. We must keep our minds from wandering far from Him at all times, turn our hearts into a spiritual temple where we would worship Him endlessly, and watch ourselves continuously so as not to do or say anything that could displease Him. When our minds are thus filled with God, pain becomes honey and solace.

I know that in order to reach this state, the beginning is very hard; because our actions must be governed by faith alone. But we also know that we can do anything by the grace of God, and God never refuses anything to those who ask earnestly. Knock and keep on knocking. I can assure you He will open in due time and will grant you in one go all He postponed giving you for years. Farewell. Pray Him for me as I pray Him for you. I hope to see Him soon.

    I am yours, etc.

Thirteenth Letter
Megan La Follett

Dear Sister,

Wouldn't it be a lovely thing, if there was a #GodFilter we could see the world through? It would be so much easier if our eyes only saw the work of God in the world, rather than having to bring our mind to focus on His presence in the noise.

Faith alone can bring us to seek Him in every moment. Faith that it will be worth the effort, trust that He will meet you there.

Willpower alone will never suffice. Our minds are too unruly, and God is far too wild for us to experience Him without being destroyed — except that He gifted us with the indwelling presence of the Holy Spirit, who can turn our faith into action.

To call a friend, what steps do you have to take? You must first have a desire to call her. Then you must dial the correct number; in other words, obey the instructions. And you must trust that she will answer the phone when she sees who is calling.

Desire. Obedience. Trust.

That is all you need to connect with God. You do not have to change your circumstances (even if you could!). You do not have to change your habits (though it can help). Wherever you are, as you are, you can choose in every moment to practice His presence.

In the beginning it can be quite difficult. The more you do it, the easier it becomes. After your friend has answered your call a hundred times, how hard is it to trust she will answer the next time? Do you have to look up her number anymore? Or do you feel constrained because only *that* number will reach her? Obedience is not a curtailing of your freedom or independence; it is simply the following of instructions to obtain a desired end result.

Do not fret about whether you are being a godly woman, a godly wife, or a godly mother. If you do find yourself fretting, don't worry about that either! Simply turn your thoughts back to God and step back into His story. Your narrative is full of surprise, confusion, anxiety, and self-absorption. His story is already complete, and you can rest in your part in it.

Where He is, there is peace.

You will make known to me the path of life; In Your presence is fullness of joy; In Your right hand there are pleasures forever.

Psalm 16:11

Selah

Fourteenth Letter
Brother Lawrence

To the same.

God knows better than we do what is good, and all He does is for our sake. If we knew how much He loves us, we would always be ready to receive from Him the sweet as the bitter, and all that comes from Him would please us. The most painful afflictions seem unbearable to us only when we see them under a false light. When we see them in the hand of God who bestows them, when we know it is our loving Father who humbles and distresses us, our sufferings will lose their bitter taste and turn into solace.

Let all our endeavors be made to know God; the more we know Him, the more we want to know Him. Since love is usually in proportion to knowledge, the bigger and deeper our knowledge of Him, the bigger our love will be, and if our love for God is big, we will love Him equally whether in pain or in joy.

Let us not fool ourselves in seeking or loving God for delicate favors He granted or could grant us. Such favors, however grand and great they might be, can never bring us any closer to God than a simple act of faith. Let us seek Him often through faith. He is within us; no need to go and seek

Him elsewhere. Wouldn't we be guilty and blameworthy if we loved Him only to care about trivial matters which He does not like and may even offend Him? These trifles might well cost us dear one day.

Let us devote ourselves wholeheartedly to Him from now on. Let us remove all that is not His from our hearts; what He wants is to have our hearts alone. Ask Him this favor. If we do all we can from our side, we will soon witness that change we long for happen. I cannot thank Him enough for the relief he granted you. I hope in His Mercy he will grant me to see Him in a few days (1). Let us pray for one another. I am in the Lord

Yours, etc.

***

(1) He went to bed and died two days later.

Fourteenth Letter

Megan La Follett

Dear Sister,

The other morning I was sitting at the breakfast table—a remarkable event on its own. The older children were off to school already, and the preschooler was ready to go. My husband was packing for a two-week work trip. The baby was in his high chair, practicing his full vocal range.

I was reading, "the root of all prayer is internal silence," and thinking, "good thing it doesn't say *external*," as my four-year-old talks about Robin and Batman and Falcon and the Avengers, laughing over Hulk's purple shorts.

Back to reading. "Contemplative prayer is a prayer of silence, an experience of God's presence as the ground in which our being is rooted, the Source from whom our life emerges at every moment."

And my son continues, "This one is black Spiderman. Is Wonder Woman an Avenger? And, Mom, does Supergirl work with Batman? Mom, who else…"

The next paragraph stops me in my tracks with relief.

"Martha's problem is not that she is busy being hostess while Mary is doing 'nothing.' Martha is self-

preoccupied and this leads to distractions and resentments that make her lose awareness of Jesus' presence. Jesus is not telling Mary to stop meal preparations, but to serve with the right frame of mind, with the right attitude, to see God in everything she does, even in the preparation of food. The 'better part' that Martha should have done was to be fully aware and attentive to the Master's presence in her home. She could have contemplated that she had the privilege to prepare a meal for the Messiah. That kind of contemplation would have been 'what is better' than the negative self-talk and percolating resentment that Martha had chosen about Mary's choice."
Dr. Michael Johnson, *Prayer: Listening to God's Voice* (Ascending Leaders, Christ Habits series)

I don't have to be Mary to dwell in Jesus' presence. I don't know where to start to even *try* to be Mary at Jesus' feet. With four young children, the mere act of sitting for longer than 30 seconds is often an impossibility.

But if I can be contemplative while my one-year-old is banging Hulk against the tray of his highchair, while I'm cooking and mediating sibling disputes, if I can have an awareness of God's presence and action *there*…I have hope.

Where He is, there is Truth.

And in that true light, we see the fullness, the absolute, the unmarred pureness of, HIS LOVE.

His lightnings lit up the world;
The earth saw and trembled.
The mountains melted like
wax at the presence of the
Lord, At the presence of the
Lord of the whole earth. The
heavens declare His righteousness,
And all the peoples have seen
His glory.

Psalm 97:4-6

Selah

Acknowledgements

This book was seeded in my heart several years ago, when I first read *The Practice of the Presence of God*. I was deeply touched by the letters of Brother Lawrence, and shocked that a monk had so much insight to offer me concerning the experience of God in the midst of the mundane. I could certainly envision myself connecting deeply with God if I had set periods of silence, reflection, prayer, and all that I imagined goes on in monastic life; it was much harder to believe I could experience that level of connection in the reality of my life as a modern-day mom. I hope that this book, with the addition of my letters, will help free you from the expectation that you must have or do x, y, or z to practice the presence of God.

 If my hope is fulfilled, it is only because of all the help I had in making it into a reality. Thank you to Ashlie Cook for the amazing cover. To Nicole Tichenor, who was the first to celebrate with me the completion of the first draft. To the brilliant Alinka Rutkowska, without whom I would still be waiting for "just" the right time to publish.

 Thank you to my husband, Jon, for making space for me; for putting up with my clickety-clackety keyboard while I typed into the night at my desk in the corner of the bedroom, and for encouraging me to commit four days to a one-woman writing retreat at a hotel with my dog. Thank you to my dog, Millie, for making sure I didn't get permanently stuck to the chair in the hotel room.

Thank you to my dad for being the first to pre-order a copy of the book—about two seconds after it went live. I'll never forget how beloved that made me feel.

Thank you to my mom for showing me how to be sensitive to hearing the Holy Spirit, and how to act with boldness and compassion at the same time. For demonstrating what it means to put others above yourself.

To my sister, Kathy, for being a living example of the transformative power of God, and for always being my cheerleader.

And, of course, thank you to each of the incredible humans who made (are making?) me a mother. Aurelia, my golden-spirited daughter. Blaise, my fiery torch of a son. Maxwell, with the imagination deeper than the deepest well. And Philip, who we've just started to know, but can't imagine loving more.

Finally, I am incredibly grateful, dear reader, for you. My prayers, however meager they may be, are with you and for you to experience intimately and richly the presence of God.

About the Author

Megan La Follett grew up in the foothills of the Cascade Mountains, where she explored her first beloved sanctuary from the back of a pony named Silver. As a married graduate student, she became a working mother to a golden-haired and strong-willed daughter. With the birth of a second child, she chose to stay at home. Two years later, another son joined the family and she began to work from home as an editor and writer. Following the birth of a third son, she joined the team at Ascending Leaders, a Christian nonprofit, as the communications lead. Her life is built on her passion for story and finding her place in the greatest story of all.

You can find her online at:

Facebook: facebook.com/meganlafollettauthor
Twitter: @megan_lafollett
Instagram: @meganlafollett
Website: www.practicethepresence.com

Letter to the Reader

Thank you for coming on this journey with me. My desire is for this book to breathe grace into the lives of mothers. If you found these letters useful in helping you experience the presence of God, I wonder if you would be willing to help share this book with other women who need more grace, where they are, as they are.

If you have five minutes today, please leave an honest review of this book. Pass the book along to a friend who is feeling like a wretched mother. Gather a group of friends who need to hear the message that God is nearer than they think, and read through the book together. You can find group discussion questions at:

www.practicethepresence.com/discuss

With love,

Megan LaFollett

Remember This

In your dark night of the soul,
He is present.

In the mob of thoughts and the "mom calendar,"
He is present.

In the past, the present, and the future – In every moment and state of your heart,
He is present

Where the noise overwhelms, and practice seems impossible,
He is present.

If you build a worship center in your heart,
you will see Him.

If your will brings your wandering mind back to God in simple prayer,
you will see Him.

When you see everything else as madness and vanity,
you will see Him.

Pursue the extraordinary in the people you meet,
and you will see Him.

In the solace in the suffering,
you will see Him.

*When you have no hope
but Jesus,*
You will see Him.

Where He is,
there is resolute strength.

Where He is,
there is peace.

Where He is,
there is Truth.

And in that true light, we see the fullness, the absolute, the unmarred pureness of, HIS LOVE.

www.ingramcontent.com/pod-product-compliance
Lightning Source LLC
Chambersburg PA
CBHW071304040426
42444CB00009B/1861